A. FRANK SMITH, JR. LIBRARY CENTER
Southwestern University
Georgetown. Texas 78626

W9-AFB-095

Oh Baby!

Oh, Baby!

Sara Stein

Photographs by
Holly Anne Shelowitz

Walker and Company
New York

To Bradley, Jason, and Adam—H. A. S.

Text copyright © 1993 by Sara Bonnett Stein
Photographs © 1993 by Holly Anne Shelowitz

All rights reserved. No part of this book may be reproduced or
transmitted in any form or by any means, electronic or mechanical,
including photocopying, recording, or by any information storage and
retrieval system, without permission in writing from the Publisher.

First published in the United States of America in 1993 by Walker
Publishing Company, Inc.
Published simultaneously in Canada by Thomas Allen & Son Canada,
Limited, Markham, Ontario

Library of Congress Catalog Card Number: 93-12677

Book design by Our House

Printed in Hong Kong

2 4 6 8 10 9 7 5 3 1

A . B . C . D . E . F . G . H . I . J . K . L . M

C
3.05.23
St340

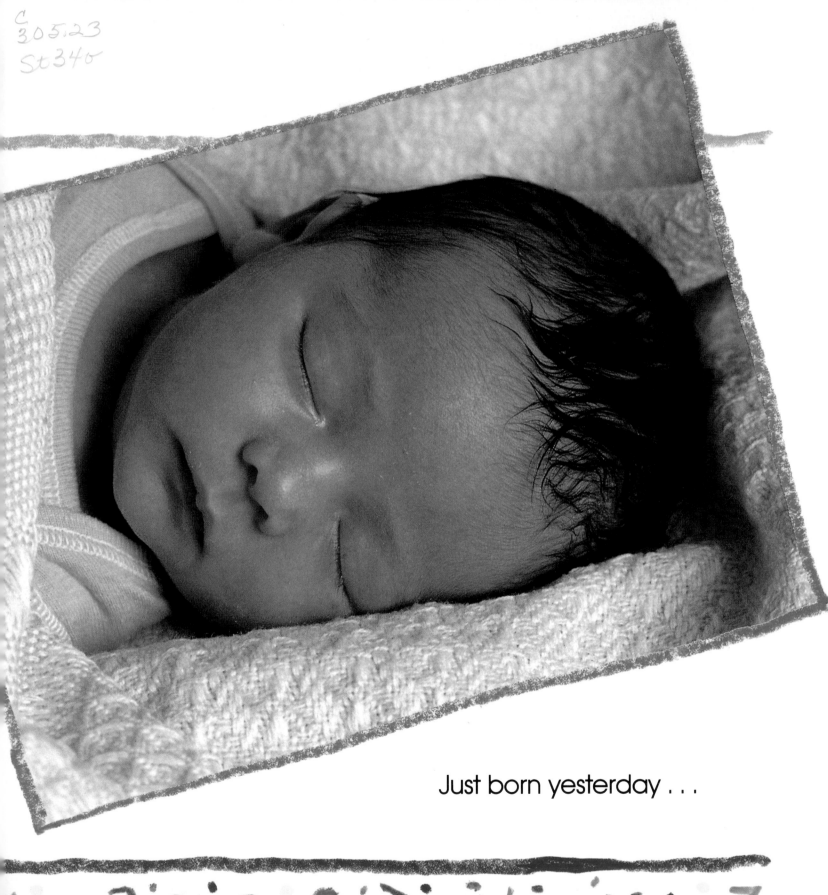

Just born yesterday . . .

N O P Q R S T U V W X Y Z

. . . and look at all the faces he can make!

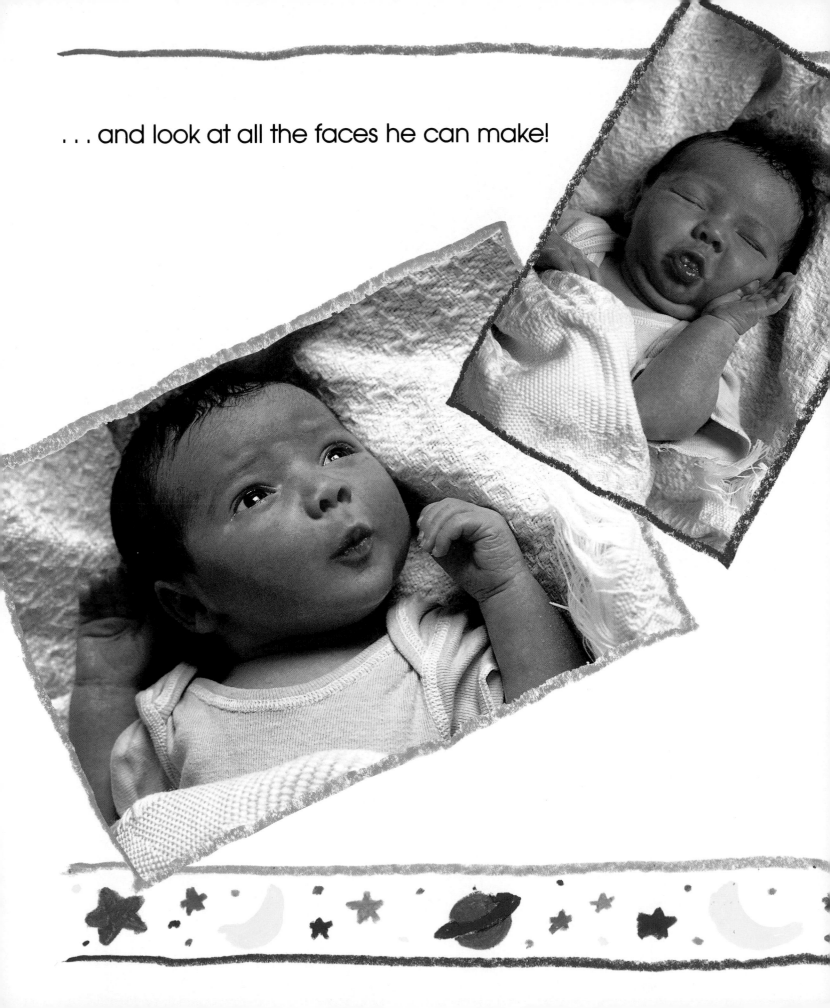

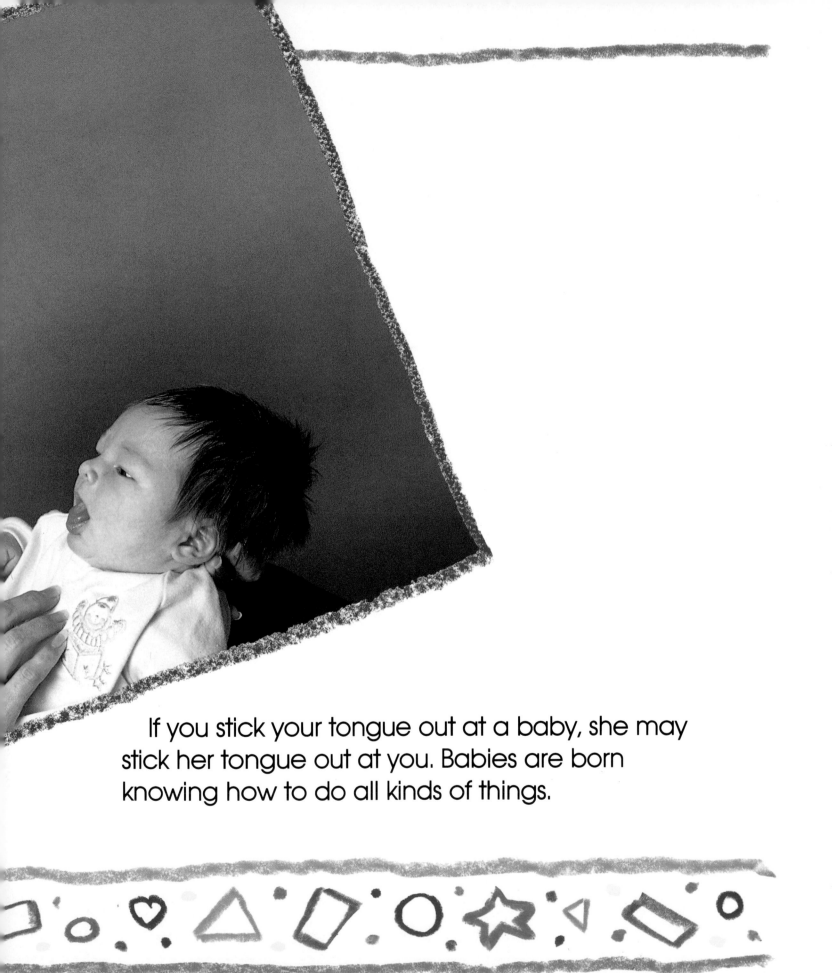

If you stick your tongue out at a baby, she may stick her tongue out at you. Babies are born knowing how to do all kinds of things.

Press a finger into his palm, and he grabs it. He tries to grasp with his toes, too.

His neck may be too weak to hold his head up,
but his fingers are surprisingly strong.

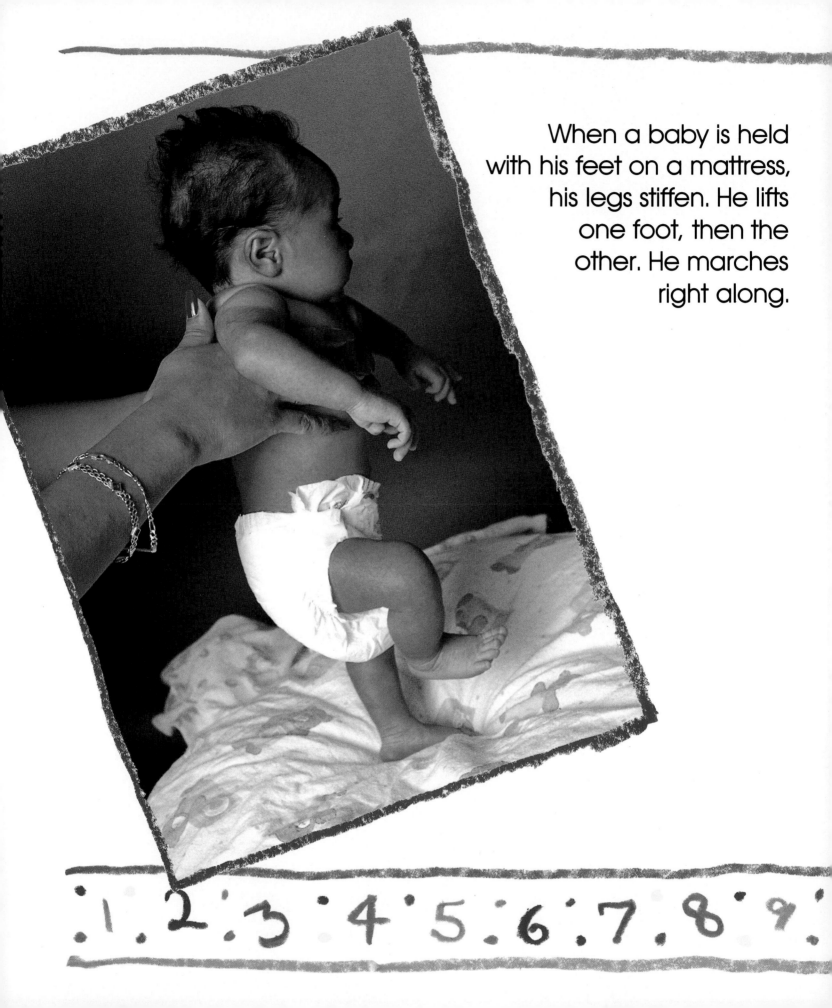

When a baby is held with his feet on a mattress, his legs stiffen. He lifts one foot, then the other. He marches right along.

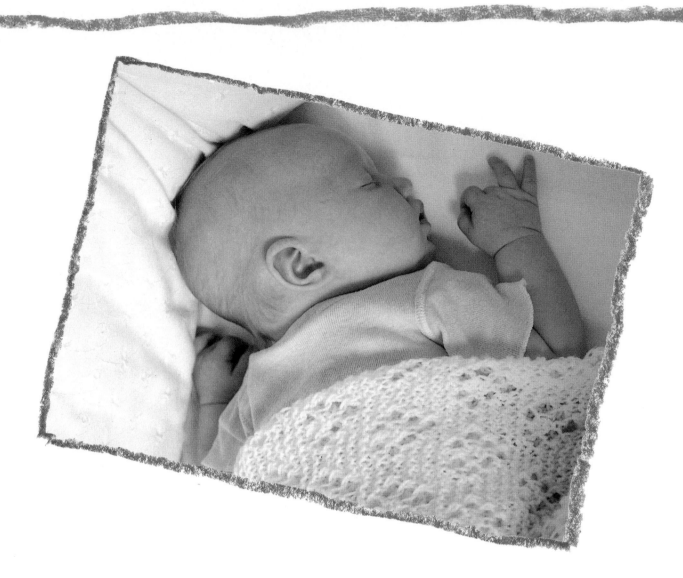

When she is put down to sleep on her tummy, she turns her face to the side. She tucks her arms and legs close to her body, scrunched up the way she was in her mother's womb. She squirms forward until she has found herself a snug nest in the corner of her bed.

Stroke a baby's cheek. If he is hungry, he will turn to your finger and suck it very hard. Some babies practice by sucking their thumb even before they are born.

A B C D E F G H I J K L M

No one has
to teach them
how to drink!

After her meal, the baby has a bowel movement. She works hard at it. It is important business. A baby needs her diapers changed about ten times a day. She will need more than four thousand diaper changes before her first birthday!

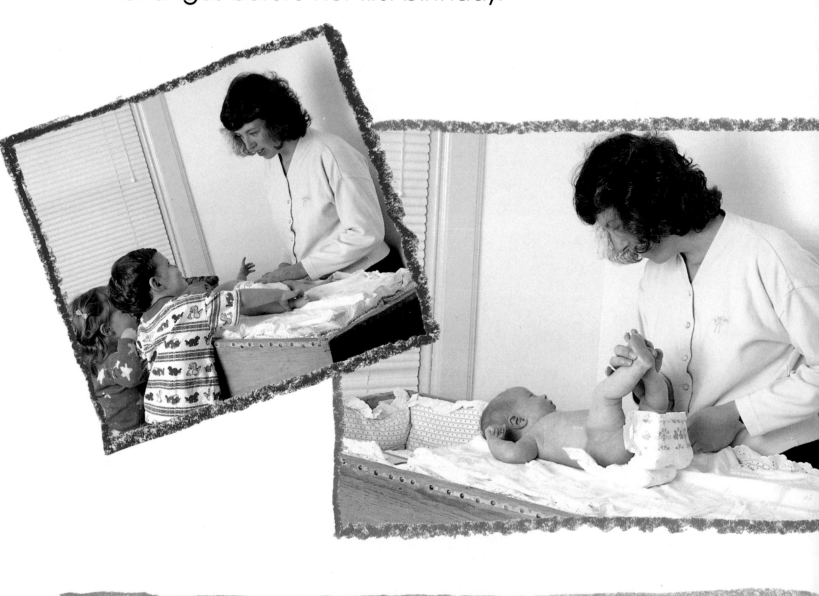

Stroking and cuddling a baby during changing and bathing help her to learn how her body is shaped and how lovable it is. Their cheeks are plump. You want to kiss them. Babies even have a warm baby smell that makes you want to sniff them.

Have a staring contest with a baby. They are very good at it. Babies stare to attach themselves to you. They hold you with their eyes.

And they catch you with their smile. Everybody has to smile when a baby smiles at them.

A baby can't take care of herself,
but she is very good at getting others
to take care of her. Her cry is a
command that people must
obey. If she is cold, they
cover her. If she is wet,
they change her. If she
is hungry, they feed
her. If she is bored,
they play with her.

As babies learn to reach for what they see, they play with whatever they can get their hands on:

noses . . .

toes . . .

everything inside their mothers' pocketbooks.

1 2 3 4 5 6 7 8 9

And whatever they can get their hands on, they
try to get into their mouths, too.

:9: 8. 7. 6. 5 :x· 3 :2 :1.

They look at the world in different ways.

A B C D E F G H I J K L M

They sit up and make things happen.

.O P Q R S T U V W X Y Z

It is a happy day when
a baby learns to crawl
up the stairs . . .
under chairs . . .

into cupboards . . .
into trouble!

They get many interesting ideas.

Remember how a baby makes stepping motions when just a newborn? Babies come prepared to do everything that grown-ups do: cry, smile, laugh, talk, stand . . .

step . . . walk!

Oh, baby! Soon you won't be a baby anymore.

1 2 3 4 5 6 7 8 9